Kyle Coare
Torn pages
Scraps of midnight

A
book
of poems

Torn Pages
Scraps of midnight

Kyle Coare

Other works by Kyle Coare.

Poetry

Prisoner of The Mind
(ISBN 978-1722975944)

Prisoner of The Heart
(ISBN 978-1731442475)

The Night Watchman
(ISBN 978-1797484419)

Seasons
(ISBN 978-1689340434)

Lone Wolf
(ISBN: 979-8613023912)

Headfirst into the storm
(ISBN: 979-8526622288)

In Shadows
(ISBN:979-8448585333)

Non-Fiction

A Brief History of Video Games
(ISBN 978-1072404828)

All available from Amazon in both Paperback and Kindle Edition

Acknowledgements

This book wouldn't have happened without all of the people that have supported me over the last 42 years.

Whether still a part of my life, or not, every soul that has touched my life has had a part to play in creating this work.

I want to thank my mother and my brother, who have always been there, listening to my mad ramblings.

To the poets that I've met across the various poetry nights in Leicester, you have all inspired me, given me belief that I can get up on a stage, that my work is worth reading. So, I thank you all so much.

To my small collection of friends that give me advice and keep me mostly sane, I would never be able to do this without you. The text messages at silly hours, the funny messages that kept me going when I was deep in editing and needed some relief.

Most of all I want to thank you, the people that read my work.
It always means so much to know that people all over the world are reading my words, watching my videos and are finding some connection with it.

So, thank you

Peace, Love and Poetry.
Kyle

ONE

Are we going to change the world?
I'll leave my blood on the page
in a heart soaked fit of rage.
Bleeding red,
to show the passion that's contained.
Can we be like a hurricane blowing through?
flattening the hurt that people do.

Her whispered name

I gaze upon beauty
in a photograph display.
Framed in words
I dare not say.
Torn page,
paper trail
show where my dreams
start to fail.
Eyes linger on the photo
encased in diamond frame.
in beauty,
her whispered name
like a lake
illuminated
by a bright moon.
I would dare the dreams
to visit me soon.
Whilst my heart lay wide awake,
my pen leaks
and the words escape,
as raindrops trace the tears on my face,
racing them to their final resting place.
I open my heart
to rainbow verses.
Nervous words inspired
by the light you provided.
By smiles that you shared.
When the sky is dark, and days feel like nights,
when all I can manage is a sigh,
I think of you
and I close my eyes.

Scraps of midnight

On torn pages
I leave scraps of midnight.
The words ripped
from the darkness
and placed
on the page in the night.
Plucked from deep within the shadows,
given their time in the light.
I leave hints of twilight,
the dusk skies,
zombies that rise,
with a deep lust
for brains
clawing out
from behind dead eyes.
On torn pages
I scatter the ashes
of my cremated heart,
the dust that settles
forming the words, I impart.
On torn pages you find old roadmaps.
Down alleys and pathways,
through the cracked
streets of my mind,
on torn pages you find
all the worlds I left behind.

Ink-stained sky

SOMETIMES it seems, that we are
Just **THE** words written in dreams.
Holding many **MEANINGS**, hidden fleeting
glimpses of reality **ARE** tied within.
The worlds may be **SEEMINGLY** ridiculous.
but they're by no means **MEANINGLESS**.
Honesty and kindness sit **THERE** eternal.
The flowing universe **IS** forever maternal,
her unwavering **TRUTH**. Love is universal.
Forever **IN** dreams, we should swim,
THE mystic rivers that dreams bring.
Life's **BEAUTY**, too short to miss.
The wonder **OF** a first kiss,
the truth in **WORDS** of love.
Sometimes kept behind doors, **HIDDEN** away,
sometimes buried deep under skin, **WITHIN**.
There is beauty in **THE** words,
the seemingly aimless **MEANDERINGS** of birds.
Magic dreamt **OF** in silken sheets.
Worlds **A** multitude, many miles away.
MADMAN or dreamer, believer in love,
away **WITH** the fairies, somewhere above.
He writes **HIS** thoughts upon clouds.
Words from his **PEN** leak into ink-stained sky.

Curse of the poet: Angry pen

My pen angrily glares.
Then starts to growl.
Ink spewing,
frothing from its
ball point mouth.
The notepad hides away,
in fear.
Letting out a
whimpered howl.
I make a grab
but I can't hold it
within my grasp.
It's squirming
and I can't clasp.
The pen shrieks
a guttural sound.
Screaming.

> *"No more.*
> *Stop wearing*
> *me down."*

Bravado heightened
by the pens outburst,
the notebook rages.

> *"Stop tearing*
> *out my pages,*
> *stop sprawling*
> *your words*
> *upon my skin,*
> *my patience*
> *is wearing*
> *paper thin."*

Floored

Lips burn like summer memories
on skin weathered paper thin.
The way a silver screen moment
can replay forever
or a split second of life sung
can live on for years.
The song in your soul reverberates
as if the whole of life is there only for
this one sweeping moment.
Where you feel your feet
and they are not touching the floor.

Soar

My heart wants to soar,
become untethered,
but its wings have been severed,
buried under 6 feet of concrete.
I paw and claw
but I'm not sure,
which will wear away first,
my fingers
or the floor.

Burst bubble

I just want to curl up
and cry.
It all feels so empty.
I want to hug myself
so tightly
I just pop out
of existence.
So tightly
I just stop
feeling resistance.
A bubble bursting into spray.
Until I'm just droplets
of reality drifting away.
I hurt inside.
I hurt in places
that are not even connected.
I feel it floating around,
a black cloud,
wrapping itself
tightly around me
like a funeral shroud.
I want to curl up and cry
under six feet of dirt piled high.
When the sun
hits my skin,
I feel nothing,
no heat or energy coursing.
When I'm bathed
in moonlight,
all I feel is the darkness
that surrounds,
not the light
that touches down.
I want to hug myself so tightly
that I stop feeling this pain inside of me.

Craggy face

Standing beside
　　this wailing sea.
　　　Stony feeling,
　　　　frail I fall.
Into memories,
　　bitter those
　　　biting winds.
　　　　Words held in hell.
　　　　　Secrets I can no longer tell.
　　　　　Stories, no longer recall.
Stood silent beside this
　　cacophonous ocean.
　　　I was so young.
　　　　A pebble on a
　　　　　sandy beach,
　　　　　　a shell that
　　　　　　　you couldn't breach.
No vessel could contain
　　my emotion,
　　　not even the shores
　　　　of this green land.
I dug my feet firmly
　　in the sand
　　　and I made a stand.
Now as still as a statue, I look.
　　The water has eroded
　　　my craggy face.
　　　　My features rugged
　　　　　and jutted out.
　　　　　　Seagulls land on my
　　　　　　　furrowed brow
and I watch the waves lapping.
　　Listen to children excitedly
　　　clapping and laughing.
I crack a smile for the first time in years
　　and flood the ocean with tears.

Questioning

I dreamt of you again.
I let you wander in.
You pulled up a chair.
Oh, where do you come from
and why do you care?
Or is this possibly all just a game?
To wear me down again
to lower my defences,
I'm questioning my senses,
but you speak so softly,
so kind and caring.
Still, could you really be an enemy
out for the kill?
Nightmare fiends
left me lacking trust.
Fairweather friends
left me to rust.
Are you here to do the same or worse?
Are you here to maim or curse?
I'm wondering too much.
Sometimes my mind wanders
through the floods.
I dreamt of you again,
last night you came to me.
You entered my dreams
through the window
in my heart,
always open, the wind blowing in.
You left a mark
that was there when I awoke.
The words you spoke,
A kiss shaped stain,
in the centre of my mind
beating down into my chest.
I wonder is this all a test.

Butterfly

That butterfly.
It stood for so much.
It's meaning hurt more
than any sharp thorny touch.
Wings would never flap again.
It wouldn't flutter on the wind
or take shelter from the rain,
but it also means
you were no longer in pain.
My heart couldn't heal you
or repair the damage done.
My hands were fighting
a battle that couldn't be won.
I thought for so long,
was there more that I could have tried
but I know in my heart I gave all I had
and that time was set like a clock
or an ocean tide.
In my thoughts
I still sit with you.
In my dreams
you are just in another room
and that brings comfort,
knowing that I can speak to you
in my hours of need,
even if its only in my dreams.

Hibernate

I want to think
of butterfly wings,
not the coldness
that winter brings.
I want the freshness
of spring,
not the harsh
winter sting.
Hibernation seems
a good idea,
just hide away
at this time of year.
Warm and cosy in my bed,
the bugs and germs
can stay away from my head.
Unless it's snowing
then winter can stay
I don't mind seeing
the majestic wonders of a snowdrop.
A moment frozen in time
but I draw the line
at this cold frozen backdrop,
where the world
feels like a rocky barren outcrop.
I want some warmth,
a soft cuddle,
a warm body held tightly.
I want a hug.
Not the slap of cold tears
as they freeze my cheeks nightly.
I want the heat
to melt those
glacial river creeks.

Head in the clouds

I may sometimes seem
like I'm gazing off
into outer space
like I'm not interested
but my mind sometimes
swirls all over the place.
Glazing over, it listens,
taking in what you are saying
but it's like a part of me
is sat elsewhere playing.

It knows it should
focus, take root,
be grounded
but it's also ever so slightly
dumbfounded
that we are not
all living up in the stars.
Instead spend more time
stuck watching traffic
from unmoving cars,
or in crowded bars,
watching life flow away.

My mind sometimes wanders,
when its flittering through my internal filing,
it may leave my body idling.
Stuttering and jittering
but my ears still hear,
my mind flutters
like a butterfly flittering,
trying to escape from the net of fear
but it knows to take in
every word I swear.

It's a little frayed and confused.
At times, it's like it's barely been used,
others it's on slowdown.
Just trying to keep itself amused.
My mind sometimes
doesn't make sense
but it takes in whole universes
that always keeps me amazed.
Whilst I stand all dazed
by a world that
I don't always
feel I belong in.
Where sometimes
the feeling of longing,
is too much to take.
Sometimes my mind
will pick me up
and put me someplace safe.

Eternal love

The stone statue
looked
longingly over
at the faded tomb
of her
long lost lover.
Alone.
Forever
she would stand.
Watching.
Waiting.
Forever.
A stony vigil.
No clocks ticking.
A solitary tear
eternally sculpted
to sombre ashen face.
Weathered.
So, the tear
is mostly faded.
Her features
long ago degraded
but her heart
never left
the place
she stood
and waited.

Glitter

Glitter shines
on frost tickled tarmac.
Ungritted lines
of ice,
raven black.
Unwritten lines,
my minds new soundtrack.
Dancing sprinkles,
dazzle
as I travel
under
the silver moons
beaming stage light.
Invigorate
the eyes,
I delight
in the sight.
The dusting
of magic
on this
cold winter night.

Stagnant tears

Stagnant tears
fill this lake.
Echoes of fear,
we cannot shake.
Lasting recollections
of yesterday.
Resemblances
of old waterways.
Where beside the waves
we would kiss
and say forever is ours,
let's keep it that way.
Severed remembrance
of everything.
Turn off the memories
that sting.
Secrets that swim,
just below the waves.
Moments to be left
to their
saltwater graves.

Rose thorn insults

If I gave you my heart
would you feed me Rose thorn insults?
That cut deep
into the pit of my stomach lining
like barbed wire. Stinging like fire.
Would you tie me up
in ribbons of derision
that would cloud my eyes,
distorting my vision.
This spiders web of frayed emotion
has me tangled.
The strands keep getting pulled,
like a jumper that is now more string
than clothing.
The jagged mangled shards
of this ice-cold broken heart
lay over the ground.
Tempting me
to try to put the pieces back together,
like a jigsaw,
only much messier.
As the ice thaws
blood still pours
and pain erupts.
like volcanic dust.
Emotions turned on and off
like a tap
but now the valve has snapped.
Yet they keep pouring.
The room filling. Flooding.
Swamped in the morning
of a last dawn chorus mourning
as the birds take to wing.
The feathery choir sing
one last song for us.

Ghostship

The
ghost ship
sails upon
the
waves
forevermore.
She follows the currents.
Avoiding the shores.
Her crew,
long since departed
to far-flung
mystic
harbours.
Now the ghost ship
Just rises and falls
with each ripple of the sea.
Listening to the seagulls
distant calls.
Floating.
Forevermore
into
eternity.

West end lights

West end lights.
With blind eyes
we emerge.
A human surge.
Up from
subsurface lairs.
Into the west end
glare.
Giant screens
advertise ways to spend,
when most are
down on their knees,
wondering how to pay the rent.
From speakers,
dance beats sound.
Energising the tiring crowd.
Street performers play.
Got to earn a crust,
make your living someway.
On these streets,
not paved in gold,
a dull lifeless grey.
The west end lights
just give them
a special shine some days.

No more

The wet whistling wind tore
through the air. Screaming, 'No more'
It said no more to all the hate,
to all the tears laid in its wake.
It ripped up trees
and smashed down fences.
Said no more
to these man-made defences.
No more.
The wild wind screamed in pain.
All the tears it had seen,
all the rage spent in vain.
All the anger and ferocity
of the human beasts
and it said no more.
No more to the way they hurt the land,
how they desert their fellow man,
The way they treat animals with disdain.
No more it said. Bringing the rain.
The wind let loose its power,
turned the waters to blood
and let the fruits turn sour.
It said no more.
No more to the constant noise,
The blood shed on the lands.
The air tainted with lead,
polluted rivers running red.
These humans need to be shown,
sown the seeds of the torment they cause,
thrown in a cell
without any doors.

Eternity

When does forever start?
I'm calling out,
yelling for that perfect moment
when love walks in from the dark.
When does eternity begin?
Will it be marked by an alarm bell ring?
Or a song that a choir will sing.
Will I even know its here?
When will all time get here?
I've been waiting for many a year,
continually waiting,
repeatedly hoping and praying,
endlessly debating,
perpetually consternating.
When is evermore
going to pass through my door?
Is it few days,
weeks
or more?
If so, I'll just sit,
wait and write for a bit.
I have no problem
passing the time.

Like the sky

She is like the sky.
Mysterious.
At times
bright and full of sunshine,
other times gloomy,
thunderous and wild.
She can be meek and mild
or furious and full of anger,
like a lightning storm
hanging over.
She is like the sky.
Quiet and peaceful
or like a hurricane
blowing through.
Hundreds of miles an hour.
She is like the sky.
Always full of wonder.
She has picture painted clouds,
they may be hearts and flowers,
other times,
there are monsters out there.
She is like the sky.
A perfect breath of fresh air
but whatever the weather above,
her heart is always full of love.

Frozen droplets

Lightly dusting
the crisp cold ground.
Frozen droplets
of water
from the guttering.
Lusty looks
before eyes
gaze down.
Leaves slowly fluttering.
I look for you
through the glistening view.
I long to see
those beautiful eyes
looking deeply
into mine.
I long to hold your hand,
tight to my chest.
Let you feel my
heartbeat race
as I gently
stroke your face.

Periphery

On the periphery,
over the river and far away.
Through green fields,
forests and towns.
Over the villages,
across the downs.
That's where I need to be.
A solitary house, that's me,
I sit on the hillside,
not in the crowds,
not like the mansion sat high in the clouds.
I'm the house that keeps
its shutters down.
Silently.
Quiet reflection washes over me.
This is where I need to be.
Away from the bustle,
the toil and hustle,
the noise and the grind,
the strain that confines
and crowds my mind.
Beyond the boundaries,
distant from castle walls.
Outside, over the moat
and far away.
Near the aching sea,
Its tearful waves,
stretching,
pulling away from me.
Just a rambler
with no land
to let his legs walk free.
Somewhere
on the periphery.

Nocturnal

A nocturnal wonderland
which so many fear
or misunderstand.
Where light
has ceased.
Night offers a feast
for the beings
too timid
to walk
busy
crowded streets.
I step through
the wall of ink,
into the
chasm of night.
Let my eyes adjust,
I let my mind
slowly think.
I regain my sight.
and to this
palace of solitude
I give my trust.
An animal nocturnal.
The howls growing internal,
hunger starts to rise.
I need to feed on inspiration,
stories and mythical rides.
I see with night vision eyes.
Keeping vigil over the night.
Watching the shadows,
eyeing the gloom
just me and
the lonesome moon.

Lullaby

Sailing on vast sapphire ocean.
The sway of the water
rocks the boat
in a steady motion.
Moon illuminating shimmering waves,
light glistening, holding tightly.
The dancing droplets that spray.
The ripples peak then collapse and ease.
Like the rise and fall
of your chest as you slowly breathe.
The rocking of the vessel
relaxes, making life less stressful
as it takes you, effortlessly by the hand,
over these open seas, it sails,
into a land
of make belief and fairytales.
The boat rises to the crest,
the breathing slower
in your chest,
as your eyelids
drift lower.
Slowing
as
sleep
gets
closer.
A faint spray of mist,
refreshes
and you enlist
all of the creatures
of the deep
to rock the boat to sleep.

Shattered stars

I bleed internally
from invisible scars.
I want to scream so loudly,
I shatter the stars.

Rise

Tongues entwined.
Entangled, twisted
around silver linings.
Sugar sweet lips,
honey drenched kisses,
as the sun blushes
and hides her eyes.
My head is in the clouds,
thinking I've died
and to heaven I rise.

TWO

Are we going to bring peace?
I'll cry my tears on this paper.
If it will ease the suffering,
Can we end it please?
Let's fight.
Not to hurt, but to heal,
not with weapons or fists
but with shared ideals.
Let's spread our thoughts with all.
Be the light.
before the darkness can fall.

Ballerina skies

Follow those snaking
silver streams.
Watch along
on glowing mystic screens.
Along shiny moonbeams,
through the great expanse,
under stars that excitedly dance.
Ballerina skies,
cloudy across the mountainous terrain.
Where nothing is quite as it seems.
Feel the pitter patter of rain,
as you slink into the arms of dreams.
Sink into their warming embrace,
as they gently stroke at your face,
wiping away the tears,
that cold water alone could never erase.
Take a breath,
listen to the soothing melody
of the midnight choirs
and close your eyes.
Feel the way your body flies,
speeding through the clouds.
With eyes closed tight, you see a new light,
a new life,
as it zooms into view.
A new world of adventure sits ahead of you.

Curse of the poet: Parchment and Quill

No longer could I
rely
upon my pen
and notebook
to get me by.
I had to change my
outlook,
or at least try.
So, out of the drawer
I took,
my quill
and parchment.
However, it quickly
dawned,
that the quill was ill
and the parchment
was worn.
No ink would spill,
my mood, forlorn.
I sunk into bed,
phone in hand.
When I noticed an app
which would
suit me grand.
So, notes, I opened
and started to tap.
The words I had
been so desperate
to write.
Now
I'm starting
to feel alright.

Descends

Freezing mist descends,
a shade of grey.
Window blinds.
The world fades away.
All of a sudden
it's like a road with no end.
Faces appear,
then disappear again.
I'm lost, shivering, shuddering
alone, in this chilling fog.
A fallen log,
in a forest of darkness,
and all I see is grey.
Endlessly tearing
the day away.

Painted beauty

Apply the brush strokes,
so delicately teasing,
they lightly uncloak,
the curves,
emotional notes,
impassioned tones.
Every word you spoke,
soaked into the oily mixture
of the paint that coats.
The paint that drips,
like kisses from soft lips.
Revealing perfect features,
hidden depths
into which the paint slips.
Every thought you let leap, blind
out of your head,
now blended into the paint that lines
the sheets of paper in my mind.

Inner child

Stop doubting yourself.
You are a poet.
A word slinger,
so go and sing,
let the verbal play begin.
Let your imagination loose,
don't worry about being too obtuse,
or too verbose,
too loquacious
or too on the nose.
Just take the words,
twist them into balls,
throw them in the air
and see how they fall.

Stop doubting yourself.
You can do this.
An empty page is not a setback,
it's a playground,
so let your inner child piggyback
on your hopes and thoughts.
Let them build old castles,
from the torn parts of your heart,
or forts
from the scars,
that you are too scared
to impart.
Let them become pirates,
sailors on the seven seas.
Feel the cold splash of water
and the sea breeze.
Taste the salt on dry chapped lips,
as you feel the first words
slowly start to drip.

Let them become adventurers,
explorers traversing
the lands of your mind,
See what treasures they find
when they dig at the place marked
with a cross on your map.
The buried memories
and the things you held trapped.
Let them breathe new life
into old lifeless toys,
things that you remember that once
brought you joy.

Let your inner child loose,
they can become
anything they choose.
Ghost hunters
in a world of haunted houses
and spooky corners.
Let them find the darkest memories
and turn them into a scary clown,
or build a new world
then flip it upside down.
Let your inner child play,
let them find the words
that you need to say.

.

Strings

I awoke. To find my heart strings
playing a symphony,
an orchestral piece,
with a joyous melody.
A lump in my throat.
I choke at the thought,
the delicious implausibility,
of someone so special as thee,
being even slightly interested in me.
I smile. A big grin that paints images
over everything.
It shows rainbows and hearts,
unicorns and fine arts
and my beating vessel
stops and starts.
Palpitations.
Palpable parallels
of apprehension,
but there is no tension.
This is just happiness
beating a rhythm inside
and the grin is painted on
big and wide.
I love. It's the only thing
that in this crazy world
makes sense.
It invents
reasons to wake.
Reasons to laugh.
Reasons to find a moment to cry.
A moment to let happy tears well up inside.
Even on those days
when your brain feels
frazzled and fried.

Stones

Pouring water over stones
doesn't soften them.
In time they
crumble to dust.
Pour love,
don't try to dampen
their edges,
smooth them out,
over time,
with soft caresses.

Leaving

The haunting piano plays
a melody that takes him
by the hand.
Leads him away,
for just a second.
To a beach bathed in sand.
Then he is back,
with a thud.
Sadly looking
over the station.
Lives floating.
Never staying.
Just passing
like a breeze,
blowing through.
Faces strained,
from the day's aches,
the gloom that seeps into you.
They don't seem alive,
like ghosts flowing to
their final resting places.
The same twisted, disjointed faces.
Their feet pound the same few feet.
Repeat and stand,
staring into nothing again.
It's unreal.
The sadness soaks you
and the ghosts continue
to flow right through.

Cliffside

A steady stream
of rainwater teems
over chiselled
features,
as
drizzled
angel tears
race,
achingly cold,
making their
impassioned embrace
with this
crumbling stone face.
The sky swirls,
angry and fierce,
reflected
in the water below.
A choppy,
charging sea.
Howling,
baying for blood,
like a pack
of angry hounds,
all bearing
down on me.
The rolling waves
crashing
in fervent
commotion.
Eroding the cliffside,
until in time,
it re-joins
the beckoning ocean.

Agoraphobic wilderness

Memories of years
in wilderness.
Such a beautiful mess.
A ballet of chaos
and distress.
An orchestra
of painful regrets
and lost years
of emptiness.
My own four wall,
desert island escape.
I passed the days
sat in solitude.
with only
my own thoughts
as interludes.
Stuttering images.
Memories
in black and white,
like watching on
old news reel
cinefilm
projector light.
Nothing felt real.
Nothing felt right.
Leaving the house
felt like an ordeal.
Leaving the house
felt like a fight.

Fireflies

Are those fireflies lighting the way?
Or are my eyes so dazzled
by the brightness of an earlier day?
Are those the dancing embers
of a passion that once burned?
Or just a lesson
I should have learned?
Does anything ever truly make sense?
Or are we just sensing
the incessant noise
of a world on the brink?
In a blink it could be gone.
In a blink. I blink
and boom. I'm alone
all of a sudden.
Are those the dancing embers
of a lost life?
Or the dust from all around
blinding my eyes?
I wish I could focus,
but the tears well up
and all I see
are waves.
I'm all at sea.
A shipwreck,
just waiting to be saved,
a capsized lifeboat
on a beach.
Salvation miles away.

Frequency

When your heart speaks
in silent whispers,
sometimes it's hard
for the world to hear,
under the constant din
of life's wheels grinding.
It's hard to hear
it faintly sing
beneath the aching
mechanical ring,
of the world stuck on fast forward.
Whilst you are freeze frame skipping,
stuttering achingly toward
the future at a different beat.
Your tune
is a frequency quite unique.

Overflowing cup

Stomach swelling.
Blood started welling.
Skin yellowing.
I'm yelling within.
Stop what you are doing.
Do I Listen? Nah, I take another sip,
and that was the final drop
that ever touched these lips.
Whiskey blended with my stomach lining,
one final time.
Enough my body screamed
and all hell broke loose.
A tidal wave of blood,
streamed from my throat,
I gurgled and choked,
and the waves kept coming.
My vision started to flood.
Months in hospital.
The outlook, they said, wasn't good.
Family told to prepare for the worst.
I'd flooded the reservoir
and the dam had burst.
Tubes in every hole.
My body no longer mine
it was spiralling out of any control.
Life slipped slowly in and out of focus.
between medically induced fever dreams,
lung bursting screams,
and tears, too many to count.
One for every drink I'd poured down.
Never once did I give up.
I fought with every drop I had left.
An overflowing cup.
My life the prize I win.
I knocked on death's door,
but he wouldn't let me in.

Wildfire

A wildfire ravages
through my emotions.
Crackling and spitting.
Embers flying,
branches splitting.
Savage and depressing,
yet impressively
mesmerising.
A devilish Inferno.
Hells own choir sing
to a crescendo.
The firestorm swirls,
a tornado of heat,
blazes to an emotional climax.
Paint warps and cracks.
Floors sag and snap.
The heat unrelenting
only devastation
does it bring.

Flowers

Flowers can bloom
in the darkest night.
Life can flourish
through the hardest plight.
Thoughts can nourish
the starving mind.
So, find the right roads
to unwind.
Untangle the crooked memories
left behind
and live the future
you hope to find.
Flowers can blossom
under a full moon.
Life can spread joy
even when you feel consumed.
Thoughts can drench a thirsty brain.
So, let the clouds bring their rain
and live the future
you wish to obtain.
Flowers can thrive
in the cold harsh hours.
Life can be so much more
if we live like flowers.

The ruined cities

The ruined cities of my mind,
crumbling to dust.
Sand on times tides,
old thoughts flow,
swaying on the waters
that flood the
ancient stonework below.
History fading away.
The ruined cities you will find
if you explore the grey matter within
streets once gold lined.
Now lay with patchwork skin.
Buildings where once sat
hope of forever,
now degraded into piles of rubble,
worn by the weather.
The ruined cities of memory,
where streets are warped.
An earthquake zone,
filled with the scattered debris
of my minds tired old thoughts.
But this is home,
this apocalyptic memory hole.
It still contains the wreckage
of my cracked and broken soul.

Dare

Dare to be
unique.
Don't sink
into the lake
of conformity.
Dare to be brave.
Comfort zones
make perfect graves.
Dare to be different.
Make your world sing
to a new frequency.
Dare to be you
in a world
that is all
Me. Me. Me.
Dare to dare.
To be aware
that you are not
flatlining out there.
So, take care
and breathe that cool air.
Dare to take big lungful's
and feel it make you whole.
Dare to take control.
Safety zones
make good hiding holes
but they hide you away
from any life at all.

Shadows of the past

Shadows of the past march by,
followed by their haunted cries.
In hobbled formation,
they wearily stumble,
towards their fateful destination
amidst the missile rumble.
Entrenched they live,
entrapped like rats.
The creeping barrage.
Dive for cover like acrobats.
Don't be alarmed.
Eyes bloodshot,
nerves turned to rot.
There is no mental discharge.
Just a court martial.

You will die today...

Either at the hands of the enemy
or your own firing squad.
The whistles blow
and off they go.
Poppies grow
Remind us that
blood flows red.
They remind us how
A generation of men were led
To the killing fields to wind up dead.
Whilst their superiors sat
drinking fine wine
and dining on meals so divine.
Not so much as a whiff
of the front line.

Sprinkled words

A distorted
litter strewn
wasteland,
all the letters
and words used,
left to fester
and disintegrate.
To wither away
into nothing
like a thawing
winter snow scene,
becoming
just slushy remnants
of old memories
and occasions
that feel
like long forgotten
dreams.
I fly over the words,
taking hold
of the ones
that I hold dear,
like trust and care,
heart and soul.
I sprinkle them
over my notepad
to keep them whole.

Walls

They are staring back.
It's disconcerting,
the way their eyes
penetrate this already
damaged
humanoid
mannequin.
They are wearing
my nerves thin.
These walls
they see everything.
They keep looking.
Deep inside.
In darkness
shadows leap
and seep into the cracks
that appear on the surface
of this empty vessel.
They wear my skin.
They listen
through concrete ears.
They know all of my fears,
they have heard the rumble
of my tears,
as they roll down to my chin.
These walls wear
the expression of distaste
on their grim
wallpaper skin.

Naked

It all drops
to the ground,
every scrap
of fabric covering.
Every garment,
hiding skin.
Every piece
of clothing,
discarded,
disrobed.
Naked now.
No longer
any barriers
or defences.
Just me.
These bare pages.
Onto which
I flood my words.
Where my pen
has let my thoughts
soak out again,
in tear-stained ink.

Morose sun

The sun sits
like a match that's been struck
but the motion
hasn't ignited it,
the fire hasn't lit.
It sits
gloomy and morose.
Almost comatose
under a gaggle of clouds,
all crowding
and huddled around.
Just checking in to see,
why the heat
has been turned down.

Time

Sometimes,
I feel like
the wisest
of men.
The rest of my life
is spent
pushing
a pull door
to open.
I mean seriously.
I can be thick,
like sometimes
my brain
is a clock,
that forgot
how to tick.

THREE

Are we going to bring love?
Can we let the world know
that although the waters are choppy,
they will one day smoothly flow.
That the distaste and anger that presides
over our towns and cities,
resides in lost quaint model villages,
will one day dissipate,
and the clouds will part.
Bringing an end to the hate,
if we all open our hearts.

Kyle Coare

Awkward encounters

My life, it seems,
has become
a series of random
internal screams and ambled walks
down streets so glum.
I have apparently lost
the ability to be human.
I ask myself what is the worst
that can happen?
And then usually that is the resulting outcome.
I've never been much of
A 'people person'
But recently my human skills
have completely left me.
I've become a boat sailing a lonely sea.
To people, I dare not speak,
They may pierce my shell
and cause a leak.
I've perfected
the rabbit in the headlight stare.
I've got so good at
blending into the shadows,
even I sometimes forget I'm there.
My lack of a voice,
the sound it makes,
like a cracked mirror as it finally breaks
in this universe of noise.
When someone has spoken
and my replying lines
are stuttered and broken.
Unable to make sense
of why my voice sits silent.
The connecting link between
brain and mouth is severed.
So, it seems that from now on,
to the shadows I'm eternally tethered.

Curse of the poet: Typewriter

Oh no, a fuse has blown...
The internet is down, so alas, no phone.
How can this writer write?
His pen and notebook,
long ago gave up the fight,
parchment and quill,
refused to let any ink spill.
And now
my phone apps are down.
Only one answer,
the poet thinks…
The old rusty typewriter.
Pulled from the cupboard.
At first the lines
are flowing well.
The perfect tool he tells himself.
But then.
The typewriter chatters
its mangled teeth,
with every heavy strike.
A sound that could
wake the dead,
or at least give them a fright.
He tries in vain
to withstand the noise,
but every key he hits,
screams in agonising voice.
It's no use, he thinks at last.
I need to get this piece
finished fast,
before the
midnight bells do chime.
The WIFI lights blink
and the Internet returns
just in the brink of time.

Angry Earth

The earth
is stirring.
Quivering.
She lets out a quake.
Explosions of volcanic rage
erupt over the land.
Anger at the state
of the life that treads
her green fields.
That covers
her in steel.
Entraps her beauty
beneath
monolith monstrosities.
Ensnares her,
forcing down
polluted air.
Angry. At the lack of care.
Angry. At the wars and death,
fought on her back day after day.
The earth is stirring.
She lets out a roar,
as she sends out tidal waves.
 "Stop destroying my costal waterways".
She screams, in pain.
 "Stop killing my trees,
 pulling down my limbs
 as you please.
 Just stop.
 And let me breathe".
The earth
is stirring.
Quivering.
She lets out a quake.
 "Let me have a little peace.
 For goodness' sake"

Brittle

Memory holed,
papier mâché facades.
Brittle
like sugar shards.
Crystalline
fragmented hearts
Smashed disjointed parts.
Sweet but deadly.
Bitter and sour.
Friend or enemy.
The lateness of the hour.

Delicate clouds
like candyfloss dreams.
Standing bold
in the sky
but blown around
they start to
evaporate and die.
The wispy heart
that can no longer cry,
finds its tears clogged
in the corner of its eye.

Fine dust,
floating bereft.
That is all that is left.
Just moments of trust
and those
words left unsaid,
left to sit
in silence
with the dead.

Fallen

With wisdom,
I'd say
that I should have
turned away.
With my mind,
I'd have run,
into fantasy
hideaways,
but instead.
I followed
my heart
not my head,
and from the edge
of a cliff,
the winds battering,
I fell.
Helplessly.
Aimlessly
into your arms
and your bed.
I wish I'd listened
to the voice that said,
stay away
from that ledge.
Don't let yourself
get drawn close.
You could end up with
much worse
than ripped
and torn clothes.

Figure

The figure,
like smoke
drifting through
the atmosphere.
Just out of view
Take a glance.
You only
catch a sight of her,
when you are unaware.
When your mind is wandering
and your thoughts
sit alone elsewhere.
That's when she appears.
Drifting by.
Floating In the air.
She will turn and smile
but her grin doesn't lie.
It's the smile of evil
and she wants you to die.
To join her in her haunting,
maybe she's just lonely
or she could just be taunting.
It's probably best
to get out of there
before she catches you unaware
and leaves you gasping,
grasping for air.

Circle

I'm a circle that doesn't fit
the square hole
into which
I am being forced to sit.
I'm a triangle,
not a foundation stone,
my angles leave
an earthquake zone,
any buildings
placed on top
will shake,
wobble and collapse.
They will break.
Into a million pieces.
A Jenga tower all over me.
I have all the wrong edges,
all splintered, split ends
Misshaped corner wedges.
I don't fit your little box,
I'm too irregular,
too twisted and contorted.
Too disjointed and distorted.
I'm a circle that doesn't fit
the square hole
you want me to sit.

Imagination

A world
without
imagination.
A truly devoid
and desolate
destination.
One through
which
you can walk
for miles.
Along baron
tarmac roads,
with
no vegetation
or
scenery
to stem
the boredom
that grows.
A world lacking
in empathy,
a place with
no dignity,
a wasteland
of nothing.
Just the land
of the empty
miserable
Souls.

Frozen fountain

Passing the old fountain,
the sound of water cascading.
The memories that spray,
long held tight inside my head.
The fantastic nights
where we chose life instead.

The water flows,
sound echoes
in those midnight moon glows.
We forgot all about fear,
we let go of pain
and let the fountain spray,
cleanse like a falling rain.
Those are the memories
that reside in my brain.

Frozen fountains,
where we danced.
Spray now stationary.
Holding its shape, for the day.
Holding my heart that way.
I remember feeling my heart burst,
exploding with so much joy.
I remember the feeling
of shooting stars,
in my universe,
deep in my gut.
Now the ice
has its frozen hold on me.

The way it stays so still.
Not moving, this bitter pill,
I want the joy to carry on,
the fountain to fill.
but beauty pulls me in.
as the sun glistens
upon the frozen surface.
Throwing rainbows
and glitter at us.

Frozen in place.
Time stands still.
My heart still beats
but at a snail's pace.
The ice will thaw, in time,
but will my heart still soar?
Or is the pen writing
it's final line.

Glimpses: Memories of yesterday

Looking at pictures.
Memories of yesterday.
Fading glimpses at the moment
when hope walked away.
Photographs of forgotten sunrises.
Sunsets burned into our minds.
Those nights.
Closed blinds.
Keeping the outside at bay.
Images contained snapshots of summer,
before the weather turned glummer.
Portraits of passion under blinding sun,
impressions of parties
drunk and out for fun.
Visions etched onto glossy paper,
Wafer thin memories
drift like translucent vapor.
Watching as summer exploded around.
The sun, the laughter
being part of the crowd.

Clown

The clown
never lets his guard down,
nor his smile slip.
Even in those times when
the brain is gripped
by intense pain.
The clown
hides behind his laughter again.

The painted smile,
never a frown.
The tears of the clown
falling to the ground.
No one realises,
no one sees through
the mask
worn
to hide the truth.

He trips and falls,
to bring joy to all,
but no one sees
the inner turmoil.
The clown,
his mask
to make you laugh.
Hides his sadness
outside your grasp.

Healing wind

Blow over me,
healing wind,
cold and brisk.
Whisk me away
to lands of bliss.
Anywhere but this
pit of worthlessness.
Moonlight,
put your arms around me.
I want to feel the beams hold tight.
I need someone to hold me now
and you are the only one I'd ever call.
Sunshine always brings about a downfall.
Cold rain
wash away this pain,
I want to feel clean.
Take my skin
if it will help to clear the stains.
I'm sick of feeling
like the only one ever to blame.
Weather me down.
Wear me out.
Trying not to drown
but it's hard,
when the river water is head deep
and your energy is sapping.
You just want to give in
have a little sleep,
done too much napping.

Mountains

Clouds sitting high.
Mountains in the sky.
Vast palatial towers,
that we can only ever climb
within our wildest dreams.
They seem
so solid and true.
Such magnificent structures
to walk through,
like cathedrals
of pure sunlight and dew.
Raid drops glisten over
the silvery view.
Oh, how magical it would be,
to walk between
the misty clouds
and the majestic sunbeams.

Lucky charms

Lucky charms
did nothing for me.
Four leaf clovers
I'd walk right over
and pick a weed instead.
I'd stick my hand deep
in nettles to feel pain,
if it would make some sense
of the thoughts in my head.
I'd rather fill my pockets
with kindness than coins.
Rather walk in rain
than sunshine,
if it will wash away
this darkness that falls,
that fills my mind,
that is so unkind.

Everlasting light

Am I hearing my song?
The one that plays
when my light is gone.
When my hope is faded
and my world
feels like it's spinning wrong.
Am I hearing it now?
I thought I'd have time
to get used to the way
silence sounds.
The way those screamed
voices have dropped out,
but now the final chords
are playing
and I've never
been one for praying.
Am I hearing it right?
Is that the music
that will lead me
away from the night,
that will guide me
through the darkness
and into some
everlasting light.

Mushroom

I see mushroom clouds
as my eyes start to close.
End times close.
Now it's time to doze.
Endless sleep
for the children of earth,
because of our own
crazy weapons of death.
I see nothing.
Black sky obliterating
the already
blood red moon.
I see waterfalls
of crimson,
red armies
of doom.
I see mushroom clouds.
I see mushrooms in fields
standing proud.
How they must look up
at the towering sight,
And think their God
has come to show them the light,
before they too
are wiped out
in the firestorm.
And I see our earth,
as she cries for her children.
Not us on two feet,
but the poor innocent victims.

Relapse

Anaesthetised.
Out of sight.
Out of my mind.
Closed eyes drift back,
slipping through
times cracks.
DJ spinning tracks.
Sipping another beer,
another shot.
Relapsed.
Got too relaxed.
Out of sight.
Out of my mind.
Closed eyes drift down
at the table,
soaked in blood,
all mine.
Prop up the bar
to stop the collapse.
Brain frazzled,
time gets lapsed.
Blue lights flash.
Siren song calling.
Down streets
we dash.
Through hospital doors
I crash.
Doctors surround
and to ten
they count,
going under,
I'm out.
Anaesthetised.
Out of sight.
Out of mind.

Precursor

Precursor to the end,
apocalyptic visions.
A world in flame.
A tornado of blame,
whirlwind of fire
and no-one left to save.
Crowds thronging
looks - cold and longing.
Something is coming.
Nightmares forming .
A looming terror,
in the air,
in the recesses of our
minds internal hardware.
Precursor to tragedy.
To the big bad entity.
Bogeyman always lurks
always prowls,
lizard lips and yellow eyes,
he howls.
The thoughts bleed
like a river
and we are caught drowning in the reeds.
Nightmares compiling
in our minds internal filing.
Nightmares sorting,
ready for reporting,
through the night.
Precursor to war.
A letter written in blood.
Words spoken in tears.
A vision appears
of demons and gargoyles,
with only one goal in mind.
To take with one hand
the living from the land.

Charged storm

A thousand bolts
an hour,
The sound
a crescendo
of crashes,
storm clouds
mass.
The downpour
here at last.
Lighting rides in on a horse,
as bright as day.
Pale moonlight,
hides the night away.
Nature
steals the show.
The night sky
Aglow.
This stunning view.
Reminds me of you,
as I hear the rain
howling at the moon.
The forceful tune.
The power
shakes the room.
Beautifully
the colours burn,
as the sky turns
blood red.

Weathered words

Words come to me
like a flurry of snow.
Drifting downwards
sentences flow,
into my head
like a sprinkle of dust.
Fine little structures
that form a message of love.
Words stream forth
like a barrage of rain.
The intense noise,
the streaks
down the windowpane.
The tears of heaven,
On full flow again.
Words blow through,
like a battering wind.
Belting me with all it can.
Making me plant myself firm,
so that I can hear the words
I need to earn.
Words shine down like sunbeams,
through grey clouds.
They give me hope.
Set free my dreams.

Slow winter snow

Live on in the words of song.
In the music that plays.
Stay, in the ether ever long.
Don't let your hope float away.
If you let your grip drop too soon,
like a child with a balloon
It will soar to the moon
and you will have nothing,
but the faded words
that you used to sing.
Hold on tightly,
to save yourself
from looking skywards nightly.
To see where your hope
now resides.
Beside the stars
on a space joyride.
Live eternally in stories told.
In memories you hold.
Forever in the atoms that flow,
in the slow winter snow,
the summer sunbeams,
autumn showers
and the spring daydreams.

Shoes

These shoes
have walked miles.
Blistered feet.
Upside down smiles.
Tear valley cheeks,
tear down walls
as we speak.
These shoes,
have worn me out.
I've been dragged around
by the scruff
of my neck.
I've been to hell
and back.
And only singed
a few loose hairs.
These shoes
that I wear,
or that wear me
Am I the wearer
Or the weary worn.
I want to feel my feet flee.
Feel like a newborn.
Free from all that holds me down,
but these shoes
have got me strolling
all over town

Sticky toffee pudding

I just want to
not feel like
a storm cloud,
like the water
going down the drain
to the sewers once again.
I want to feel like sunshine,
or a steaming mug
of tea,
a warming hug
against the cold rain,
that's all I want to be.
I want to feel like
sticky toffee pudding.
Complete with lashings of custard.
I want to make you
lick your lips
and say that was good.
I don't want to sour the mood,
though I often do,
because sometimes,
it's hard to get my sunshine
to warm through the clouds
I've become accustomed to.

Hopes in a basket

Some say
I put all my hopes in one basket,
but sometimes hope
is all you have left.
It will probably leave you feeling bereft,
but all you can do is lay it out,
or lay back
and bask in its
endless
cycle of lies.
You see,
hope is the worst feeling in life.
At least with rejection you know,
It's a sharp kick,
a heavy blow
and down you go.
Able to count away
the moments
as recovery, although slow,
is already
starting
to
happen.
Hope is a different animal.
Hope keeps on saying,
it could be okay,
long after you have lost,
even when being guided
through purgatory,
hope will probably say
that recovery
is mere moments away.

Teacher

I still see you,
in every wisp of the clouds.
Every drop of dew
on the ground.
Every footstep
I hear the sound,
your voice soft
but the words
strong and loud.
I can feel the way you hugged me.
Even though it was hard for you
to let emotion free.
You let the birds sing,
let them take to wing,
you cared, you fed the foxes at night,
you shared your heart and your light.
A teacher
of everything.

Candy kisses

Popping candy kisses.
So passionately
two mouths entwine.
Lips tingle
with each brush.
Every touch
sends electricity rushing
up the spine.
Outside becomes
a blur and birds
sing a chorus line.
Two sets of eyes gazing
in amazed anticipation,
feeling the sparks,
this exciting sensation.

Pulled close.
Two bodies
breathe as one,
like an ocean
those waves
ripple upon.
Lingering
sherbet kisses
touch the softness
of skin,
fizzing lips
share the
excitement
within.

Fingers dance
through candy floss hair,
across delicate chin,
around the nape of the neck,
between shoulder blades,
angel wings should protude there.
Down the back.
Softly painting
a message of love
with each delicate stroke.

Holding on tight
as the sunlight fades.
Soft wisps of perfection,
in the shades of the dusk light glow
Rainbow drop waters wash
over the two bodies
fading into the bed below.
Moonlight dances
slowly through the dark,
two souls embark
upon a life of dreams,
as they hold close,
breathing in time.
Two perfectly aligned stars
in a vast cosmos
of chaotic hearts.

The abject object in my room

Within these confines, I confide,
to my four walls, I cried to them,
so many tears. Too many to hide.
I am
the object
in my room.
A thing,
not worth
much,
just a commodity
to be used up.
Took away years,
this cell without bars
The walls don't have ears,
they just
hold my scars.
Every scrap that I tore,
every shred that I store,
in paper torn
and ripped,
on the floor.

Relax

Relax your mind.
Let yourself unwind.
Find comfort
in the veil of night,
as the light
slowly leaves.
Pull your covers tight.
Hold on to your head,
the rides about to begin.
Keep your hands within.
Lay still
let your breathing slow,
as the carriage takes you higher still
and sends you
passing through
dreams of fun,
lost memories
of days in the sun.
Let sleep
take you to
Places you
want to view
Let the dreams
be your
tour guide
On a magic carpet ride
and when you land,
sink into the soft caress
of their warm hands.

FOUR

Can we really change the world?
Dispel the curse, remove the hurt,
with just some words and verses
Can we spread hope?
Give the world purpose.
We must try.
Let our thoughts amplify.
passing on hope
to stem the tears that cry.

Sanity

I often question my sanity,
sometimes it answers back,
gives me anxiety,
the hate filled voice
that speaks through the cracks.
Imparting thoughts
with bile and menace.
Yelling at me that I'm vile and horrendous.

I often question my sanity,
with thoughts about how different I seem.
How difficult it is to make sense of a daydream,
how I can't feel happy in company,
unless it's my own little team.
My thoughts reply
in tones that horrify,
that I'll always walk alone
that I'm way too shy.

I often question my sanity.
In moments of vanity,
when I look in the mirror
and don't hate the reflection I see,
it answers with a snarl,
snide and raspy.
That I'm not thinking rationally,
that I shall never amount to much.
I don't have the luck or the look.
My mind is a worn out, ripped up book.

I stopped questioning my sanity,
The answers it gave
were filled with negativity.
Started to love
the person that I am.
The frayed edges
need no apology,
the care I give,
the love I share.
Mean more to me
than just dead air.

Youth

How dare those youth have such fun?
Don't they know this was all fields
when I was young?
We didn't have access to the Internet.
A world wide web
wasn't something we'd dreamed up yet.
It would paint images in our heads
of spiders spinning threads.
We didn't have phones that went everywhere,
Pocket sized links to the world out there.
We only had corded wonders,
rotary phones,
why were the emergency services
the hardest number?

We didn't have
fancy computers
No laptops
for commuters.
2 colours on screen
at any time
and sounds that resembled a wet fart
(Still better than grime)
They struggled to play a simple game,
tic tac toe,
would cause fuses to blow
and flames to rise,
like hades in a heatwave,
when the sun has decided to explode,
and this is all after spending 10 minutes
waiting for the game to load.

Don't know they are born,
this bunch of millennial spawn.
Our media was physical,
no storage clouds,
ours didn't float around.
Films on cassette tapes.
Music on vinyl,
spinning
as the needle scratches away.
Laser disk promised
so much,
but to own one
you had to sell your mum,
your grandma
and a part of your soul.
So we made do with VHS
and holding fast forward,
we had no remote control.

Street signs

Following street signs
no direction in mind.
Just reading the words,
following the lanes.
To see what we find.

Blindly driving,
headlights
slicing
into rain.
Diving forward
across bumpy,
treacherous terrain,
never looking back again.

For behind
is where
we leave ghosts
in the dark.
Tortured pains
that rip through your heart.
We leave those
soul breaking howls,
that swirl through your head.
The moments of terror
where you think
you'd rather be dead.

The dark mist descends,
and the road just ends.
Disappears into the grey.
Won't appear again today.
Through the coldest
of winds
and the harshest
of rains,
with the fear
you lose your head
along with your brains.

Climb

I can't seem
to climb
out of this hole.
Down deep
where hands
can't reach.
I'm so far from safe
that I've forgotten
how it feels,
So far from awake
but I've forgotten
how to sleep.

I feel defeated.
I'm beaten,
can't seem
to get a grip.
My fingers slip.
Just breathing seems
too much trouble.
I see no solution
in the surrounding rubble.
All I can do is sit tight,
through lonely days
and long nights

Can't keep going,
I'm losing
and its showing,
like the hole
I'm deep in,
my mind
overflowing.

Ripped fabric

A rip in the fabric,
reality splits
in two.
Broken mind feels
lost to you.
Here comes the storm.
The swarm
buzzes through.
Here comes
the morning.
When I am
lost in the blue.
A rip in the fabric,
A tear in the seams.
Nothing is ever
all that it seems.
When we are
looking for answers,
but only questions
do we find,
are we working with
half a broken mind?

Dusk

Dusk falls over dense woodland,
orange to deep purple and blue,
then jet black,
to eyes that view.
Dark green trees mix and blend,
morphing into colours and shapes
too difficult to comprehend.
Birds circle and sing
for the final time tonight.
Silhouette trees
like monsters that pry,
tear apart the moonless sky.

Just outside of town,
the small house sits alone.
No neighbourly companion
or outhouse to bemoan.
Just trees for company
and a patio, weeds overgrown.
The chimney spits smoke
up high, it billows,
mixing with the clouds,
light flickers in the window.
A candle to ward off the hoards
of demons from below

Inside sits a grizzled man.
His heart torn to bits,
shaking he listens
to the sounds,
his knuckles cracking,
as the night throws a fit.
But the noises are not the one
he wants to hear this night.
Wishing for just a single sound,
however slight.
A voice,
that hasn't been heard in years.
He wipes away freshly wept tears.

But this one night,
a voice does come.
It speaks in a whisper, 'time is up'.
Not the voice
he wanted to hear,
not the sound
of his love come near.
This a voice
which comes to us all.
He tiredly smiles,
as the scythe does fall.

His last thought.
Now he can rest in peace,
beside the woman
that put him at ease,
that made his life
feel complete.
Before she was taken
by that awful beast.

Aghast

Aghast.
Lonely planet
after the fallout.
The world eerie quiet.
The rubble of the aftermath,
shadows of history carve dark paths.

Wreckage
strewn around.
Where man walked,
now quiet dead towns.
Darkness cutting like a knife.
No summers here in the afterlife.

Silence,
once golden.
Now just deafens.
Only the rustling winds
ripping through the steel graveyard.
The sound of a dead planet.

Rebirth.
New bloom
seedling breaks through.
Soil contaminated can't abate.
Won't stop life taking shape.
Time is all, just need to wait.

Ink splattered night

Look into the roaring,
orange flames.
The dancing embers,
swirling heavenly.
Cold air, shivers.
Smoke hangs heavily.
Delivering a view,
explosions of colour.
Ink splattered sky.
Gunpowder residue.
The sounds,
a war zone,
rockets
and carnival tunes.
Through smoky grey
a faded figure
Stands upon burning
Pyre,
as the flames lick
higher and higher.
I think,
should we celebrate
the killing of men
that wanted religions to integrate.
That wanted
to not see their families killed in hate.
Just because of their beliefs.

Loving ghost

If I could be your lonely ghost,
I'd be the one that loves you the most.
A poltergeist floating around your house.
I'd tie together strands of paper,
to form a message that is true.
A chain of letters,
that spell out 'I love you'.
I'd hover to the kitchen,
and make you a brew.
I'd cook a dinner,
set the table for two.
I'd be there, invisible,
but I'd be in the air.
Dotting around items
to show you that I care.
If I heard angry voices,
or a nasty chorus of words,
I'd throw around the pots and pans,
be sure to disturb.
I'd always float around,
whenever you want me to.
I'd lay and cuddle quietly,
even though I'm see through,
I'd make sure you always knew,
the way you made me feel.
I'd write it on bathroom mirrors,
for when the steam does fill.
I'll be your lone ghost,
always pottering around,
I'll float through the house
and never make a sound.

Dust and ashes

The dust and ashes.
Scorched earth patches.
Rebirth of old pain,
trauma seeps into withered skin
and it starts to take hold again.
Reinvigorated with new flowers
to soak with its poisonous acid rain.

All the human wreckage
and emotional wasteland,
that once made the man.
Detritus on storm-ravaged sands.
Clay from which anxiety can mould
whole new countrysides to dissolve.
Whole new ways
to make its presence known,
to have its story told.

Like slurry rivers
it flows thick and slow,
into veins and arteries
under the placid skin below.
It poisons the wells and pollutes the ground.
Now given a new life, it starts to surround.
It clings to every inch of land,
to every tinge of life.
It sucks you dry,
leaves you cold
just asking yourself why.

Unfair funfair

Fortune teller.
Story seller,
your future
will be told.
You will go home poorer,
and I'll be
swimming in gold.
You need hearts
of diamond,
wishes
of crystal kisses.
Sharpened glass beads
formed under pressure,
from hearts of coal.
To emerge from this
insane funfair whole.
This life, the rollercoaster we ride,
we can see spectators at the side,
it has only one stop.
It has many hills and troughs,
highs and lows,
slow points
and fast galloping flows.
We need to have wits of iron,
steely resolve
As the waltzer cars spin.
Dizzyingly spiralling
we grip tightly to the ice cold safety,
of the knowledge that this fear is only temporary.
Amusements and games
show the charade
for what it all is.
Smoke and mirrors. There are no winners
Just the players and the played.

Wanderers

Wanderers of the sky.
Planets to you or I.
Distant places.
We would need
a rocket ship,
to take a trip
to visit in situ,
the places you view.
Behemoths of the sky.
Taunting the stars to align.
Telling us stories
of constellations
throughout time.

Hearts and flowers

Hearts and flowers,
chocolates and sweets.
Loves lasting treats.
Like a magic spellcaster
you have me stuck firmly in place.
Ever faster and faster,
my heart starts to race.
Hearts and flowers,
I remember the hours,
when I would pine away,
wishing you were mine to stay.
To love and hold,
against the harsh winters cold.
As I dreamt
of your beauty
and the magic spells
you foretold.
Hearts and flowers,
true love towers
high above,
like skyscrapers
kissing the sky.
Where the moon sits
looking beautiful tonight
and reminding me
of you and I
holding tight.

Old scars

Reconnecting with old scars,
how I held you so close,
Remembering those
days. I let them stay.
In the words on my page,
not to cage but to free,
To let your spirit turn
from pain to one of beauty.
I painted you a heart in words.
To comfort, give kindness.
To gently stroke the hurt from within.
With every brush of my tearful pen.
I wanted to ease the wounds,
So, I wrote them in verse,
gave them a home.
Their own private universe.

Peasant on the fire

Jeeves!
Throw another peasant on the fire,
us reptiles need extra heat.
Stoke the funeral pyre.
Let those flames beat.

Lizard skin flaking,
snakes in high places.
High stakes
the choices they are making.
Hissing in our faces,
pretend that they care,
but we are just numbers.
Statistics
under computer
screen glare.

Chameleon,
blends in.
Hiding in plain sight,
eyes darting from left to right.
Changing their looks to suit the mood.
Changing suits to fit the stage.
They pretend our interests are theirs,
but we are just figures,
they don't want to engage.
Just ones and zeros
marked upon a page.

Sandpaper

I pick up my pen
and start scratching
letters over the page.
Spidery little blotches,
indecipherable even to me.
Is this a new language
or is it just hurt
and pain unleashed?
I keep going,
the ink ever flowing,
spills out like tears wept.
Tears that crept
down these cheeks.
Nightly for weeks,
months, years.
These tears.
They mix
with the black ink
leaving an imprint
on the paper.
Like sandpaper
it tears at my fingers,
they bleed.
A whole new thing
to bring to the page.
Blood, tears and ink
spill in rage.
The words start
to take shape.
The page becomes
a flurry of motion,
I see images,
feel emotions
that I try to draw
in words.

Waterfall

To walk in the wilderness,
in the backwoods, deep in the shrubs.
We would kiss near the foxglove,
beside the place
where roses bloom.
Make love under waterfalls,
as the ice spray
cools hot skin.
Passions burning. We would give in.
Two hearts touching,
as they beat together.
Holding tight.
Bound as close as any tether
could bind.
The forest air invigorates as we breathe.
As naked tangled bodies intertwine,
becoming like the roots underneath
this lush green carpet,
on which we lay.
So perfectly soft,
so perfect to share
this special day.
Holding each other tight,
as our lungs stop trying to fight
and relax.
No need for masks.
we have only each other in view.
No one else to interrupt,
no rude interlude.
Just us and the trees,
the waterways
and the gentle
stroking breeze.

Morning train

A morning choir of birds
singing just for us.
The dawn adorns us with
its tuneful chorus.
Over the sleepy horizon
stretches the waking sun. Yawning.
Ready to bring the day to everyone.
Still sleepy commuters
and suits, wide awake,
stare intently at computers.
Cornflakes
down white shirt.
Startled
waking up with a jerk.
As the voice
on the tannoy yawns
the names of towns.
Coffee and soap
scented air
rains
down
on the early
morning
train.
Rush to work,
join the hustle.
Cattle led
to the markets bustle.
The sleepy eyes
brought to life
as the city lives, breathes
and thrives.

Dance like a candle

She moves
like a candle dances.
Twirling
in the darkness.
Circling me.
I'm stood enchanted,
her dress slips
like the sultry hot wax that drips.
She sends
a kiss through
the air.
It floats,
an ember,
a scorched reminder,
a passionate kiss
from her fiery red lips.
Like a feather on the air,
it lands tenderly.
I let my heart feel its heat,
as it burns deep inside of me.
And with that
she disappears.
A wisp of smoke.
Fading
into the rooms
gloomy air.
As the feeling
disappears,
left with just a
warm wet cheek
from all the tears that leak.

Moonlight stretches

Moonlight stretched out
over the
glorious landscape.
Breath-taking beauty,
no photograph
could replicate.
A fantasy draped
in dim nightlight.
My heart beat
fights to keep me alive.
As I fall into arms
of satin silk skin.
A dream as beautiful
and serene,
as a waterfall
under a rainbow,
in an idyllic
landscape scene.
And I'm the happiest
I've ever been.
Every single songbird singing
in perfect harmony.
Tantalising sounds
echo across
the mountains and valleys.
And in front a sight
only for my eyes to see,
the view bathed in the scent
of fruit and blossom trees.

Fear and feeling

A flurry of nervous words
and sweaty palms.
His mind hurried,
he tries to calm.
He tries to focus,
but his head is worried.
He tries to choke the voices
spinning a whirlpool up there.

How could anyone want this,
he thinks,
the chains
in his mind,
start to chink.
He hears the key
in the lock again,
as the padlock wrapped
around his heart
is clicked shut,
and then.

He hears the chains
grinding.
He hears a clink
and he can't fight.
He feels the grip
around his chest,
getting tight.

He fears the feeling
that his lungs
are not breathing right.
That nothing is working quite
as it should do.
He fears the feeling of leaving,
he feels a fever of pain rushing through.
He hears the key
and the door flings open.
He fears leaving.
So, inside will have to do.
And he fears the feeling,
the free-falling failing,
of falling fatally
in love with you.
He fears the feeling,
that free-falling failing,
of a solitary room,
he fears the sound
of his heart giving up,
he feels the fear flow through.

He hears the key.
Then it clicks.
The lock breaks.
He hears his breath.
He feels his chest rise and fall.
He is outside.
Walking.
Proud and tall.

Trickle of time

Trickle of time,
down it falls.
Little hand turning.
Slowly crawls.
As the hours
of yearning
barely move at all.

Time passes
Slowly,
like pages
turning.
Taking an eternity.
Feels like
Forever,
like being
stood still
in atrocious weather.
It just dawdles
forward,
been here
so long.
Waiting for
a call
but it's been
just a minute.
Sixty brief seconds,
that's all.

Time sleeps,
night creeps by,
like a shadow
over the land.
When you are waiting,
watching
the turning hands.
You focus
on the falling sands.
Legs go numb
from sitting for too long.
All you want
is to stand.

Time stopped.
Did I drop the clock?
Did I pull the plug?
Or break the hours
like a dropped glass block.
Imagining time
like a river that flows.
Now just a trickle,
hitting a dam
that slows.
I wish
for an hour with you.
A day,
a week,
a year or two.
I wish for eternity.
Instead of a river
I want our time
to be a sea.
Not a meandering stream
that stops ever so suddenly.

Black cloud

The black cloud
hasn't so much
as floated over me,
it's anchored itself
over my turbulent sea.
It's fixed itself
above my sails.
Raining down
big lumps of hail.
It's cancelled
all appointments
and changed
all of my plans.
It's taken all
of my notes,
scattered them
to the wind.
The black cloud
hasn't wandered in
from a long night away.
It's been with me
for many a day
but now
it's taking
centre stage.
Annoyed at being
misrepresented
or left off the page.

Destructive

I float through
surveying the scene.
Crimson thoughts
and sinful dreams.
Painted images
on display,
below where my wings
take residence today.
I look over.
The devastation,
the annihilation,
like a page straight
from revelations,
and I close my eyes,
hoping that not seeing
will make it untrue.
Will undo
the destruction,
you saw to pursue.

Paint a story

Let me paint a story,
the images blur,
they twist and they turn,
until a narrative occurs.
A tale of hope and of love,
contained within
a paint splattered frame.
A picture
with no name engraved.
Just a still mirage
in natures elements.

Let me paint
you a picture.
A vision of beauty.
A still life
I'd always viewed
as an image
too good for me.

She walked in moonlight,
her footsteps
more like
skipped joyful
flights.
She danced
on the air,
barely making
an indentation
on the ground,
and never a single
footstep sound.

She flowed,
like a steady stream,
through day and night,
right into my dreams.
Where she stayed.
Forever and a day. Never strayed.
The threads were never frayed.
To keep me company,
whenever I close my eyes
on nights of moonless skies.

Solitary

In
solitary
bliss
I walk.
Spring
in my step
like memories
of that first kiss.

I
walk
through
lush green grass.
It brushes
fingertips,
as I
stroll past.
I feel
the strands
like fine
long
hair,
as I
slip away
into dreams
of
those trips
we shared.

I
walk
solitary
footsteps,
wind
in my hair.
Raindrops glisten
on cobblestone streets,
where our hearts
were swept.
Sunlight
glinting.
Music leapt
into my heart.
and then
the dream
slowly falls
apart
when I realise
that in it.
You are
not
there.

Forgotten generation

Are we
the forgotten generation?
left to feel unloved
by our nations.
Untouched
by the waves of elation,
that swept through past celebrations.
It's like we are stumbling,
headfirst Over a cliff,
the rocks crumbling,
into a vast empty pit.
No money, no hope
no change, no chance
no future.

Are we
the lost generation?
We see the hurt caused by our nation.
The wrongful notion
that colonisation
made us a greater civilisation.
Where owning land,
people and their belongings,
was not seen as theft,
or enslavement,
but as our right.
How did any of these
people sleep at night.
Are we the lost travellers
of these empty pastures?

Do we just dig through the dirt?
Like archaeologists of hurt,
trying to find some fragments,
that show any worth.

Chaos

All the chaos
he keeps inside,
whirlwind thoughts
may seem unkind.
Disorganised
fractured mind,
Ruined by
the tracks of time.
The hastily bolted
framework lain,
Too warped
and buckled,
for this emotional
freight train.
Steamroller thoughts
destroy all
that get in their path.
Self-destructive aftermath.
Set to forward, no instant replay,
no brakes to slow,
crush all in their way.
Cyclonic cycles
of synapses firing,
none of them in sync.
Not linking,
each one
slowly retiring.
Sinking.
Until the eyes
are left glazed over.
Merely blinking.
No life inside.
Just a brain
Being dragged along for the ride.

Hunger

Hungry,
he hunts, lonely as night.
Prowling
under blood red skies.
He howls,
growling
as the moon sighs.
Dead silence.
Hears only his
heartbeat pounding,
Footsteps
and his last hope drowning.
Yellow eyes reflect.
Shining
like two golden
suns rising.
Aching
Inside.
Just need to feed.
A scrap
of meagre seeds
would be
as satisfying
as roast beef,
but in this
wilderness,
all is
emptiness,
like his stomach
lined with
nothing
but pain
and regret.

Library

A land of worlds
to walk through.
From floor to ceiling,
universes into
distant memory
or alternative reality.
Twisting corridors,
of musty old tomes,
roads to Paris,
Istanbul and Rome.
This place
is everywhere,
all at once.
A world where science
and fantasy become one,
or can battle
until eternity does come.
Where dragons can breathe fire,
and on Mars we can breathe.
Once inside
It's hard to leave.
The tales of make belief
and the real stories
of our history,
will hold you glued
to your seat.

Leaving train

The leaving train
Waves,
farewell.
Breathe.
Swallow
the lump down
deep
in your throat.
Feels like
you are about to choke,
as the
falling leaves
stain the ground.
The engine
whirls,
wheels turn,
stomach churns
as the end is just a foot away.
Saying farewell
with a wave.
The leaves tell tales of autumnal days.
Orange
and brown.
They fall.
Please stay.
The leaving train
Departs.
Station left in pouring rain,
leaves turn to mush again.
Tears frame
your face
as hearts collapse
and fall apart.

Heartbeat in eternity

Just a heartbeat in eternity,
one note out of history.
A single footprint
on forevers long sandy beach.
The first accent of a peak,
we feel unable to reach.
That one small step,
It's always the hardest.
That leap of faith,
into the darkness,
but the prize is a life,
instead of a living death.

Swerve

Don't let the pain
infect your heart.
Cold and harsh,
the landscape
so dark.
Don't fall apart.

Some things
are unfair,
It's not always
about you
or how much you care.

Don't walk in saddened fields,
where shadows reach out
trying to steal
A touch,
a feel
of your heart,
left so brittle.
Small
lost terrified.
So little.

Feeling unreal.
unwell wont heal?
Don't paint a universe
of all that brings hurt,
Swerve the bad thoughts
that sink in like dirt.
If it makes you feel worse
just give yourself love,
all that you can hold,
let it cover
like rainfall from above.

Extinguish bad notions,
Angry flames doused
by happy oceans.
Let them go.
floating away
Smoky wisps
from an unmade grave.
Somewhere inside
where light fades
and hope sits awaiting,
another downpour of rain.

Metamorphosis

Like a low flying airplane,
I can hear it coming.
The roar of the darkness,
hurtling forward towards me.
In tireless devotion
to devour me whole,
consume me within
its black hole of conformity.
Become
the mindless automaton
it wants me to be.
Controlled
like a puppet master
has me by the strings.

The darkness engulfs me,
like the wings of a goth butterfly
or a jet-black sea.
I sigh.
Too tired to cry,
Too hurt inside
to swim to safety.
I let it swallow me.
Deep
in the belly of the beast,
I encounter the remnants
of old forgotten feasts.

I cocoon myself,
to protect the remaining
strands of my already frayed
and tethered
mental health.
I cocoon myself,.
to give me a chance
to flourish again.
Once I've taken
hold of the pain,
torn it up and threw it
deep into the acid pit
of the beast's digestive tract.
I make a pact, with myself.
To look out for my health.

Sounds fizzing and crackling,
like lightning bolts
coursing through.
A pure white light.
Blinding.
Dazzling.
Flows through the cracked prism
of my soul. A rainbow.
All the colours aglow,
metamorphosising
through the spectrum,
shining love
deep into my heart.
I have you
and this forged,
stirred molten heartbeat,
to warm me through.
So, I'll emerge
from my cocoon anew.

Twisted shifting gears

Another gear clicks into place,
the twisting sound
of metal upon metal
and thud. The bolt drops.
Another layer
to my mental block,
safety lock.
Another padlock
on the door of my sanity.
You can knock,
but I won't let you In.
This time the door
stays shut.
Closed tight.

Becoming more distant.
Vacant signs
say there is no one here,
but I'm here,
just vacantly vacated,
the building is clear.
My body just a shell.
I'm stuck,
in the room,
in my head,
controlling
the whole shebang.

Emotions. Turned off.
Face flat.
Smiles at...
Dogs and cats.
Check.
Everything else is being left
on autopilot.
The barriers
have gone up.
I have fires
to put out in here.

Sometimes I need to be distant,
to make it bearable
to share a room.
I can't seem to do
the whole human thing,
I try,
but fail to speak,
I try to exhale
the words just sort of squeak
and crack
into splinters.
My mind sits
juggling the pieces.

Go quickly, to bed

Go quickly to bed!
Pull that duvet over your head
and become one with the dark.
Let your energy recharge,
as you sleep through the night.
Until morning light enters your eyes
and you wake feeling bright.
Go quickly I said!
Stop reading these verses.
If you don't get sleep quick
I'll get blamed and cursed.
Go quickly to bed!
Before the clock
starts to chime,
turn off your night light
and enjoy your dream time.

Thank you for reading.
If you have enjoyed this book
then please leave a review
where purchased.
Peace, Love, and Poetry.
Kyle.

ALSO AVAILABLE

Prisoner of the Mind
ISBN 978-1722975944

"The prison of the mind
A cell, darkness, confined
So many souls, filled with dread
Chained and shackled, to the thoughts in my head"

This poetry collection touches on battles with mental health issues, depression, anxiety, self-harm and addiction.
It delves into the dark parts where mental and physical illness meet.

"Smooth and lyrical, Kyle Coare's Prisoner of the Mind is like a glimpse of bright sun awakening in a forgotten cell. It is a fresh ray of hope burning through a mire of despair, and yet it also acknowledges its darkness openly, without fear or shame.
swift and powerful like a tribal drumbeat.
Prisoner of the Mind is a work of pure tears, love, and crimson with blood. I feel it will resonate with many readers, if not indeed every reader in one way or another. I highly recommend it with a solid 5 out of 5 stars."
Realistic Poetry International

Prisoner of the Heart
ISBN 978-1731442475

"Here sits the prisoner of the heart
Frozen in place, so wishes to depart
To explore the lands outside these four walls
The city of love, his destination calls"

This poetry collection broaches all aspects of love, from the highest peaks to the deepest depths.
Take a tour of the prison of the heart, let it embrace
Feel your heartbeat race, just beware there is no escape

"Sombre and melancholic, at times, Author Kyle Coare is overcome by the wildly, withered, growing weeds infesting his delicate heart as it is stripped of some of the most important nutrients needed, such as love, trust, and light, to endure some of life's harshest, cold seasons. The variation of emotions throughout the collection naturally reiterates the theme of this book, effortlessly, and is, honestly, realistic! And not just when it comes to the tender heart of Author Coare. With this, we are extremely pleased to present this book with a 5-star rating and believe it is great for either soul; the one locked inside their own heart...or for the one who holds the key!"
Realistic Poetry International

The Night Watchman
ISBN 978-1797484419

"When day ends, and night falls
When the sun leaves the sky, and darkness calls
The watchman sits, his duty to observe
Protect the dreams, of those who deserve"

This poetry collection takes us on a journey into the murky depths of the night. Down dark alleyways, through disused wastelands.
The beasts are out in force, who will hear our calls?
it will be a long night, but the watchman is looking out for us all.

"The Night Watchman is a thought-provoking carousel of dreams, rage and sympathy all at once. Rebellious but kind-hearted, powerful and fresh. A relevant collection to current problems.
It is an observant and raw book of poems that I would recommend for anybody with a full five stars. If you need proof that poetry is just as vital, if not more vital to literature today than it's ever been, here is proof."
Realistic Poetry International

Seasons
ISBN 978-1689340434

"Seasons keep turning, like the hands on a clock
tick tock, the pendulum rocks, as we take stock
days pass, the weather changes on the fly
spring into summer, a gull cries into autumnal skies"

This thought-provoking poetry collection touches subjects ranging from love and loss to addiction and mental health issues.
Taking a tour through the seasons.

"Author Kyle Coare is an exquisite Poet and Word Artist that truly knows how to bring words and the world to life through poetry, and this collection of animated poems is more than proof!
Reader's will experience the rush of each season while traveling through its pages, from summer to winter, to spring to fall, in which we realize just how well life and people mirror the concept and cycle of the seasons and how they change. This book is one of our favourites from the Author. Kyle Coare is both an artist and a poet in this collection, creating specially for the heart, mind, body, and soul. Beautiful work."
Realistic Poetry International

Lone Wolf
ISBN 979-8613023912

"Wolves howl, they don't cower from the storm
they prowl, they don't crawl or fear the swarm
the lone wolf takes a step from the pack
But don't stand too near, he's ready to attack
Snarling, his teeth glint in the moonlight
The pale spark of hope in the night"

Join the wolf on his path, as he tries to make sense of the world, we inhabit. Seeking answers in the aftermath of a wrecked planet. Through the urban wilderness of love and hurt, anxiety and mental illness. Against the backdrop of an apocalyptic nightmare world, on the brink of collapse.

"It is very apparent that many heartfelt efforts went into this book; the author bares their heart on their sleeve. Thus, we do believe that many reader's hearts will be equally captivated – just as much as ours were. the style of writing which is seen within Lone Wolf seems quite unique and refreshing. Collections like these are a rare breed, and we recommend adding this one to your shelves as soon as possible"
Realistic Poetry International

Headfirst into the storm
ISBN 979-8526622288

"The rain poured like we had angered the gods
thunder roared lightning struck the brick and stone facades
of the halls that we sat, enclosed inside
nowhere else to hide
we heard the drumming downpour
and we bunkered down fortified"

Feel the cold chill of fear, the icy sting of pain as we run
headfirst into the rain, through a year that never was,
2020 its given name.
Embark on an emotional joyride, let the weather guide
ducking and diving for cover as the driving rains fall
we search for calm trying to find the sunshine after the storm.

"This poetry is rooted solidly to the ground, emotionally reaching down
to hell, but at the same time with moments that can lift the soul.
it could easily be a modern-day Decameron. With 105 poems about life,
mental illness, virus, lockdown, lost love, failed relationships and more
than the odd political and social commentary that lays it on the line.

This is no nonsense, powerful poetry, written to be spoken, not shouted
from a podium, maybe at speaker's corner to get attention or from be-
hind a news desk, because folks what's here is real, it's happening and
we have a responsibility to listen, understand and act."
Carl Butler (Dark Poetry Society)

In Shadows
ISBN:979-8448585333

"Something is coming,
its hiding in the dark.
In shadows, it is stalking,
ready to stop your heart"

This poetry collection will take you deep into the bowels
of hell, Through its lava filled mouth, where demons howl.
217 pages of horror themed poetry storytelling.
Filled with humour, scares, light and shade.

"Kyle has once again left us spellbound and on the edge of our seats
with this tantalizing collection. The various forms of proses and poetry
take us through the innermost workings of the unexpected ride that is
life. Your mind and soul will dance in grace and reverie, as you move
through its pages. This incredible title is immersive, in every aspect.

"In Shadows" is an exquisitely crafted masterpiece — a micro adventure
that is a delight to experience; don't delay! If you're looking for material
built with genuine care that can offer soft introspection and the thrill of
discovery, this latest treasure from Kyle is the book for you!"
Realistic Poetry International

ABOUT THE AUTHOR

Kyle coare is a poet and author from Leicester, England.
When he was young, he dreamed of writing but as is so often the case real
life got in the way. He suffered with addiction and mental health problems
until they almost took his life. Spending lengthy spells in hospital.
after recovering. He became reclusive, hiding from the world.
Roughly ten years later, in a fit of self-loathing and introspection, he decided
to put his pen to paper and start trying to find out who he was,
one word at a time.

Now he writes daily, often shining his light on mental health or society.
He tries to combine poetry and storytelling, with some humour and some
dark edges, but is just as comfortable writing about love and hope, as he is
loss and hurt. His work can be dark, but through the darkness there is always
light. He has performed at various spoken word events and slams and is the
2022 2funky/Some-Antics slam winner. His work has also feature on the
BBC website.

www.facebook.com/wordsandfluff
Https://linktr.ee/wordsandfluff

Printed in Great Britain
by Amazon

17824034R10088